Bryan Cranston: A Journey Through Acting, Adversity, and Achievement

In the bustling streets of Hollywood, on March 7, 1956, a star was born. Bryan Lee Cranston, destined for greatness, would carve his name into the annals of acting history through his sheer talent, versatility, and unwavering dedication.

Bryan's roots were firmly planted in the soil of show business. His parents, Annalisa "Peggy" and Joseph Cranston, themselves actors, laid the foundation for his eventual ascent. But life wasn't always glamorous for young Bryan. His father's departure when he was just 11 cast a shadow over his childhood, forcing him to confront life's hardships at a tender age.

Raised in Canoga Park, Los Angeles, Bryan found solace in the embrace of his maternal grandparents on their poultry farm in Yucaipa, California. It was here that his resilient spirit began to take shape amidst the trials of a broken family and financial instability.

In the midst of adversity, Bryan discovered his passion for acting. From his humble beginnings at Canoga Park High School's chemistry club to Los Angeles Valley College, where he pursued an associate degree in police science, Bryan's path seemed destined for a different trajectory until an acting class sparked a revelation. At 19, the course altered the course of his life, igniting a fire within him that would fuel his journey to stardom.

Armed with determination and a hunger for success, Bryan embarked on his acting career. From local theaters to the bright lights of Broadway, he honed his craft, weaving his way through a myriad of roles that showcased his depth and range as an actor.

The turning point came in the late '80s when Bryan's persistence bore fruit. Roles in soap operas, commercials, and voice acting laid the groundwork for what would become his breakout moment. It was his portrayal of Dr. Tim Whatley on "Seinfeld" that propelled him into the spotlight, setting the stage for his meteoric rise.

But it was Bryan's portrayal of Hal, the bumbling yet endearing father on "Malcolm in the Middle," that endeared him to audiences worldwide. The show catapulted him to sitcom stardom, earning him critical acclaim and three Primetime Emmy nominations.

However, it was his role as Walter White in AMC's "Breaking Bad" that cemented Bryan's status as one of the greatest actors of his generation. His transformation from a mild-mannered chemistry teacher to a ruthless drug lord captivated audiences and critics alike, earning him a slew of awards, including multiple Primetime Emmy Awards and a Golden Globe.

Beyond the small screen, Bryan's talent transcended to the stage and silver screen. From his Tony Award-winning performance as President Lyndon B. Johnson in "All the Way" to his riveting portrayal of Howard Beale in "Network," Bryan's versatility knew no bounds.

Yet amidst the glitz and glamour of Hollywood, Bryan remained grounded, using his platform to champion causes close to his heart. From his advocacy for child safety to his philanthropic endeavors, Bryan's generosity knew no bounds.

As the curtains close on one chapter of his illustrious career, Bryan Cranston's legacy continues to shine bright. From the streets of Hollywood to the stages of Broadway, his journey serves as a testament to the power of resilience, passion, and unwavering dedication. And as he takes his final bow, the world awaits with bated breath, eager to witness the next act in the saga of Bryan Cranston, a true Hollywood legend.

As the spotlight dims and the curtain falls on one chapter, Bryan Cranston's journey is far from over. With each accolade and achievement, he continues to redefine the boundaries of his craft, leaving an indelible mark on the world of entertainment.

Following the triumph of "Breaking Bad," Cranston's career soared to new heights. From captivating performances in blockbuster films like "Godzilla" and "Argo" to lending his voice to animated classics like "Kung Fu Panda 3," his versatility knows no bounds. With each role, he breathes life into characters, infusing them with depth and nuance that resonate with audiences across the globe.

But it's not just on screen where Cranston shines. His foray into literature with his memoir, "A Life in Parts," offers a glimpse into the man behind the characters. Candid and introspective, the book delves into Cranston's personal journey, from his humble beginnings to the pinnacle of success.

Yet, amidst the glitz and glamour of Hollywood, Cranston remains grounded, using his platform to shine a light on causes close to his heart. From his advocacy for child safety to his unwavering support for social justice, he embodies the true spirit of philanthropy.

As the years go by, Cranston's influence only continues to grow. Whether he's captivating audiences on stage, gracing the silver screen, or lending his voice to a worthy cause, his impact reverberates far beyond the confines of the entertainment industry.

And so, as the final act unfolds, Bryan Cranston's legacy endures. A testament to the power of passion, perseverance, and the unwavering belief in the transformative power of storytelling. For Bryan Cranston is more than just an actor; he is a beacon of inspiration, lighting the way for generations to come.

With each passing year, Bryan Cranston's influence continues to transcend the boundaries of time and space. His name etched in the annals of Hollywood history, he stands as a paragon of talent, resilience, and unwavering dedication.

Beyond the glitz and glamour of the silver screen, Cranston's impact resonates in the hearts and minds of fans worldwide. His portrayal of complex characters, from the enigmatic Walter White to the indomitable Lyndon B. Johnson, has left an indelible mark on popular culture, shaping the way we perceive and understand the human experience.

But Cranston's legacy extends far beyond his on-screen accomplishments. A tireless advocate for social change, he lends his voice to causes that matter, using his platform to amplify the voices of the marginalized and disenfranchised. From championing LGBTQ+ rights to advocating for environmental conservation, Cranston's activism serves as a beacon of hope in an ever-changing world.

As the years roll by, Cranston's star only continues to rise. From his electrifying performances on Broadway to his captivating roles in blockbuster films, he defies the constraints of age and genre, proving that true talent knows no bounds.

Yet, amidst the adulation and acclaim, Cranston remains humble and grounded, a testament to his enduring humanity. Whether he's mingling with fans on the red carpet or sharing words of wisdom with aspiring actors, he never loses sight of the values that have guided him on his journey.

And so, as the curtain falls on another chapter in the illustrious career of Bryan Cranston, one thing remains abundantly clear: his legacy will endure for generations to come. For in the tapestry of Hollywood history, his name shines bright as a symbol of excellence, inspiration, and the timeless power of storytelling.

In this era of fleeting fame and momentary trends, Bryan Cranston's legacy stands as a towering testament to the enduring impact of genuine talent and integrity. As we gaze into the future, it's evident that his influence will extend far beyond the confines of his filmography, inspiring not just future generations of actors but anyone who aspires to make a difference through their art and actions.

Cranston's journey from the humble beginnings of television commercials and guest spots to becoming an emblem of cinematic and theatrical excellence embodies the quintessential American dream. It's a narrative that speaks to the possibility of transformation, not just of the self but also of the roles one inhabits. In doing so, Cranston has become a beacon for those who dare to dream, encouraging countless individuals to pursue their passions with relentless perseverance and an unwavering commitment to their craft.

Moreover, his willingness to explore the depths of the characters he portrays, to find humanity in even the most flawed individuals, challenges audiences worldwide to look beyond the surface. Cranston's characters often navigate moral ambiguities, reflecting the complexities of real life and inviting viewers to engage in introspection and dialogue. This nuanced approach to storytelling has not only elevated the quality of entertainment but has also contributed to broader cultural conversations about ethics, morality, and the human condition.

In the realm of philanthropy, Cranston's contributions underscore the profound connection between art and activism. By leveraging his fame and resources, he has shone a spotlight on critical issues, reminding us of the power of celebrity influence for societal good. His endeavors serve as a call to action, encouraging others in the entertainment industry and beyond to use their platforms for positive change.

As we look to the future, the blueprint that Bryan Cranston has laid out for an impactful career in entertainment continues to inspire. It's a blueprint that emphasizes the importance of versatility, the courage to tackle challenging subjects, and the significance of giving back to the community. His career serves as a reminder that while roles may come and go, the impact of one's work on society, the messages conveyed, and the lives touched, remain forever.

In conclusion, Bryan Cranston's enduring legacy is not merely a collection of his roles and accolades but a mosaic of his influence on culture, society, and the individual lives he has touched. As an actor, philanthropist, and human being, Cranston embodies the idea that true greatness comes from the heart's ability to empathize, inspire, and transform. As we continue to witness his journey, one thing is certain: Bryan Cranston will be remembered not just as a remarkable actor but as a catalyst for change and a symbol of timeless excellence in the world of entertainment.

In the annals of Hollywood history, Bryan Cranston's name is etched not just as a performer, but as a maestro of his craft, orchestrating symphonies of emotion and intrigue with every role he embodies. As the curtain rises on each new chapter of his career, Cranston continues to captivate audiences with his magnetic presence and unparalleled talent, reminding us of the transformative power of storytelling.

What sets Cranston apart is not just his ability to inhabit characters with depth and authenticity, but his relentless pursuit of excellence in every aspect of his craft. From his meticulous preparation for each role to his unwavering commitment to pushing the boundaries of his own abilities, Cranston embodies the spirit of artistic dedication and innovation. It's a commitment that has earned him the adoration of fans and the respect of peers, solidifying his place as one of the most revered figures in the entertainment industry.

Yet, for all his achievements, Cranston remains grounded in humility and gratitude, never forgetting the journey that brought him to where he stands today. Whether he's accepting awards on stage or engaging with fans on social media, he approaches each interaction with authenticity and humility, embodying the values of integrity and kindness that have guided him throughout his career.

But perhaps Cranston's greatest legacy lies in the impact he has had on those around him – the aspiring actors inspired by his journey, the fans moved by his performances, and the countless individuals whose lives have been touched by his philanthropy. As a mentor, philanthropist, and advocate, Cranston has dedicated himself to paying forward the opportunities he has been given, ensuring that the next generation of artists has the support and guidance they need to succeed.

As we reflect on Cranston's storied career and the indelible mark he has left on the world of entertainment, one thing is clear: his influence will endure for generations to come. Whether through his iconic performances, his philanthropic efforts, or his unwavering commitment to excellence, Cranston's legacy serves as a beacon of inspiration for all who dare to dream.

And so, as we applaud Bryan Cranston for his remarkable achievements and celebrate the impact he continues to have on our world, we are reminded of the power of passion, perseverance, and the relentless pursuit of greatness. For in Bryan Cranston, we find not just an actor, but a symbol of hope, resilience, and the enduring power of the human spirit.

In Bryan Cranston's journey, we find a story of resilience, perseverance, and the triumph of the human spirit. From his early days as a struggling actor to his meteoric rise to fame, Cranston's path has been marked by challenges overcome and obstacles conquered. It's a narrative that resonates with audiences around the globe, inspiring countless individuals to pursue their dreams against all odds.

But Cranston's story is not just one of personal success; it's also a testament to the transformative power of art. Through his performances, he has the ability to transport us to worlds both familiar and fantastical, inviting us to explore the depths of the human experience and discover truths about ourselves and the world around us. Whether he's portraying a high school chemistry teacher turned drug kingpin or a beleaguered president fighting for civil rights, Cranston's characters are imbued with a complexity and nuance that challenge us to see the world in new ways.

Yet, amidst the accolades and applause, Cranston remains grounded in his values and his commitment to making a positive impact on the world. His philanthropic efforts, advocacy work, and dedication to giving back serve as a reminder that true greatness is measured not only by one's achievements, but by the lives they touch and the difference they make in the world.

As Bryan Cranston continues to write the next chapter of his storied career, we can only imagine the heights he will reach and the impact he will have. But one thing is certain: his legacy will endure for generations to come, inspiring future artists, activists, and changemakers to follow in his footsteps and strive for greatness. For in Bryan Cranston, we find not just a talented actor, but a beacon of hope, resilience, and the power of the human spirit to transcend any obstacle in pursuit of a dream.

In the tapestry of Hollywood's history, Bryan Cranston's story emerges as a shining thread, woven with passion, perseverance, and unwavering dedication. From his early days of humble beginnings to his ascent to the pinnacle of success, Cranston's journey is a testament to the transformative power of talent and tenacity.

With each role he embodies, Cranston transcends the confines of the screen, breathing life into characters that resonate deeply with audiences around the world. Whether he's portraying the morally complex Walter White in "Breaking Bad" or the charismatic Lyndon B. Johnson on Broadway, Cranston's performances are imbued with a rare authenticity and depth, leaving an indelible mark on the hearts and minds of viewers.

But Cranston's impact extends far beyond the realm of entertainment. Through his philanthropic endeavors and advocacy work, he uses his platform to shine a light on pressing social issues and lend his voice to those in need. From supporting children's safety initiatives to championing environmental conservation, Cranston exemplifies the transformative power of using one's influence for the greater good.

As he continues to chart new territories and explore uncharted realms of creativity, Cranston remains guided by the values of integrity, humility, and empathy. His unwavering commitment to his craft, coupled with his genuine compassion for others, sets him apart as not just a formidable talent, but a beacon of inspiration for generations to come.

As we eagerly anticipate the next chapter of Bryan Cranston's illustrious career, one thing is certain: his legacy will endure as a testament to the enduring power of storytelling, the resilience of the human spirit, and the boundless possibilities that lie within each of us. In Bryan Cranston, we find not just an actor, but a true icon whose influence will continue to shape the world long after the final curtain falls.

In Bryan Cranston, we find a luminary whose brilliance illuminates both the stage and the screen, captivating audiences with each nuanced portrayal and inspiring countless hearts with his unwavering commitment to excellence. His journey, marked by triumphs and tribulations alike, serves as a testament to the transformative power of passion, perseverance, and the relentless pursuit of one's dreams.

As Cranston continues to push the boundaries of his artistry, he remains steadfast in his dedication to using his platform for positive change. Whether he's lending his voice to social causes, mentoring aspiring artists, or simply leading by example with his integrity and humility, Cranston epitomizes the notion of an artist as a catalyst for social progress.

But perhaps Cranston's most enduring legacy lies in the hearts and minds of those he has touched along the way – the aspiring actors emboldened by his journey, the fans moved by his performances, and the countless individuals inspired by his acts of kindness and generosity. In every interaction, Cranston radiates a warmth and authenticity that transcends the confines of fame, reminding us all of the power of empathy, compassion, and human connection.

As the story of Bryan Cranston continues to unfold, we are reminded of the profound impact that one individual can have on the world. Through his artistry, his advocacy, and his unwavering commitment to making a difference, Cranston serves as a beacon of hope and inspiration in an often tumultuous world.

In Bryan Cranston, we find not just a masterful actor, but a true luminary whose legacy will endure for generations to come. And as we look to the future, we can only imagine the heights he will continue to reach and the lives he will continue to touch, leaving an indelible imprint on the world and reminding us all of the boundless potential that lies within each of us.

In Bryan Cranston, we find a luminary whose brilliance illuminates both the stage and the screen, captivating audiences with each nuanced portrayal and inspiring countless hearts with his unwavering commitment to excellence. His journey, marked by triumphs and tribulations alike, serves as a testament to the transformative power of passion, perseverance, and the relentless pursuit of one's dreams.

As Cranston continues to push the boundaries of his artistry, he remains steadfast in his dedication to using his platform for positive change. Whether he's lending his voice to social causes, mentoring aspiring artists, or simply leading by example with his integrity and humility, Cranston epitomizes the notion of an artist as a catalyst for social progress.

But perhaps Cranston's most enduring legacy lies in the hearts and minds of those he has touched along the way – the aspiring actors emboldened by his journey, the fans moved by his performances, and the countless individuals inspired by his acts of kindness and generosity. In every interaction, Cranston radiates a warmth and authenticity that transcends the confines of fame, reminding us all of the power of empathy, compassion, and human connection.

As the story of Bryan Cranston continues to unfold, we are reminded of the profound impact that one individual can have on the world. Through his artistry, his advocacy, and his unwavering commitment to making a difference, Cranston serves as a beacon of hope and inspiration in an often tumultuous world.

In Bryan Cranston, we find not just a masterful actor, but a true luminary whose legacy will endure for generations to come. And as we look to the future, we can only imagine the heights he will continue to reach and the lives he will continue to touch, leaving an indelible imprint on the world and reminding us all of the boundless potential that lies within each of us.

In the ever-evolving narrative of Bryan Cranston's life, we witness the unfolding of a remarkable odyssey characterized by resilience, artistic brilliance, and unwavering commitment to craft. As the chapters continue to unfurl, Cranston's journey serves as a testament to the enduring power of passion, perseverance, and the relentless pursuit of excellence.

With each role he inhabits, Cranston ventures into uncharted territories of the human experience, deftly navigating the complexities of emotion, morality, and identity. From the harrowing depths of Walter White's descent into darkness in "Breaking Bad" to the towering presence of Lyndon B. Johnson on the Broadway stage, Cranston's performances transcend mere acting, becoming profound explorations of the human soul.

Yet, amidst the accolades and acclaim, Cranston remains grounded in humility and authenticity, never losing sight of the values that have guided him throughout his journey. Whether he's engaging with fans, mentoring aspiring artists, or using his platform to advocate for social change, Cranston embodies the principles of integrity, compassion, and empathy in all that he does.

As the story of Bryan Cranston continues to unfold, we find ourselves captivated by the profound impact he has had on the world around him. Through his artistry, his philanthropy, and his unwavering commitment to making a difference, Cranston serves as a beacon of inspiration for generations to come, reminding us all of the transformative power of storytelling and the boundless potential that lies within each of us.

In Bryan Cranston, we find not just a master craftsman, but a visionary whose legacy will endure far beyond the confines of the silver screen. As we eagerly anticipate the next chapter of his journey, we are reminded of the timeless truth that greatness is not measured by fame or fortune, but by the lives we touch and the legacy we leave behind. And in the tapestry of Bryan Cranston's life, we find a story of hope, resilience, and the enduring power of the human spirit.

In the grand tapestry of Hollywood, Bryan Cranston's narrative emerges as a vibrant thread, woven with brilliance, passion, and a relentless pursuit of excellence. With each step he takes upon the stage or before the camera, Cranston paints vivid portraits of humanity, breathing life into characters that linger in the collective consciousness long after the curtain falls.

As his journey unfolds, Cranston's story becomes a testament to the transformative power of perseverance and dedication. From his humble beginnings to his meteoric rise to fame, he navigates the highs and lows of the entertainment industry with grace and resilience, inspiring countless individuals to chase their dreams with unwavering determination.

But Cranston's impact extends far beyond his performances. Through his philanthropy, advocacy, and mentorship, he uses his platform to uplift others and effect positive change in the world. Whether he's supporting children's charities, championing environmental causes, or lending his voice to social justice movements, Cranston exemplifies the notion of a true artist as a force for good.

As we continue to witness the unfolding chapters of Bryan Cranston's journey, we are reminded of the profound influence that one individual can wield in shaping the world around them. His legacy serves as a beacon of hope and inspiration, encouraging us all to strive for greatness and leave a lasting imprint on the world.

In Bryan Cranston, we find not just a consummate performer, but a guiding light whose brilliance illuminates the path for generations to come. And as his story continues to unfold, we eagerly anticipate the next chapter in this extraordinary saga of talent, passion, and boundless possibility.

In the ever-evolving saga of Bryan Cranston's life, each chapter unveils a new layer of depth, resilience, and creative brilliance. From his formative years to his ascent to iconic status, Cranston's journey is a testament to the enduring power of passion, perseverance, and the unwavering pursuit of excellence.

As the spotlight follows Cranston's footsteps, he breathes life into characters with such authenticity and nuance that they become indelibly etched into the fabric of popular culture. From the enigmatic Walter White to the formidable Lyndon B. Johnson, Cranston's portrayals transcend mere performance, offering profound insights into the human condition and sparking conversations that resonate far beyond the confines of the stage or screen.

Yet, amidst the acclaim and adulation, Cranston remains grounded in humility and empathy, never losing sight of the values instilled in him by his upbringing and experiences. Whether he's engaging with fans, mentoring aspiring artists, or using his platform to advocate for social change, Cranston exemplifies the transformative power of using one's influence for the greater good.

As the narrative of Bryan Cranston's life continues to unfold, it serves as a source of inspiration and empowerment for countless individuals around the world. His journey reminds us all that success is not merely measured by accolades or achievements, but by the lives we touch and the legacy we leave behind.

In Bryan Cranston, we find not just a consummate actor, but a beacon of hope and resilience whose story inspires us to dream boldly, live passionately, and embrace the limitless possibilities of the human spirit. And as we eagerly anticipate the next chapter of his extraordinary odyssey, we are reminded that the greatest stories are often those that are still being written.

With every new chapter in Bryan Cranston's journey, the narrative deepens, revealing layers of complexity, triumphs, and profound moments of introspection. From his early struggles to his meteoric rise to fame, Cranston's story serves as a testament to the resilience of the human spirit and the transformative power of perseverance.

As he continues to captivate audiences with his compelling performances, Cranston transcends the boundaries of mere acting, embodying characters with such depth and authenticity that they resonate long after the final credits roll. Whether he's portraying the morally ambiguous Walter White or the indomitable Lyndon B. Johnson, Cranston's portrayals are imbued with a raw honesty and emotional resonance that leave an indelible mark on the viewer's psyche.

But Cranston's impact extends far beyond the realm of entertainment. Through his philanthropy, activism, and unwavering commitment to social justice, he leverages his platform to effect positive change in the world. From advocating for children's safety initiatives to championing environmental causes, Cranston embodies the principles of compassion and empathy in all aspects of his life.

As we continue to witness the unfolding chapters of Bryan Cranston's narrative, we are reminded of the power of storytelling to inspire, uplift, and unite us in our shared humanity. His journey serves as a beacon of hope for dreamers and believers everywhere, a reminder that with passion, determination, and resilience, anything is possible.

In Bryan Cranston, we find not just a talented actor, but a true visionary whose legacy will endure for generations to come. And as we eagerly anticipate the next installment in his remarkable saga, we are reminded that the greatest stories are those that continue to unfold, inviting us to embark on a journey of discovery and self-discovery alongside one of the greatest storytellers of our time.

As Bryan Cranston's narrative unfolds, each chapter reveals new layers of his humanity, resilience, and boundless creativity. From his humble beginnings to his towering achievements, Cranston's journey is a testament to the transformative power of passion and perseverance.

With each role he undertakes, Cranston immerses himself fully, breathing life into characters with such depth and authenticity that they become indistinguishable from reality. Whether he's embodying the complex anti-hero Walter White or channeling the commanding presence of Lyndon B. Johnson, Cranston's performances resonate on a visceral level, leaving an indelible impression on audiences worldwide.

Yet, beyond the glare of the spotlight, Cranston remains grounded in humility and empathy, using his platform to champion causes close to his heart. From advocating for children's safety to supporting environmental conservation efforts, Cranston embodies the values of compassion and social responsibility in both his professional and personal endeavors.

As the tapestry of Cranston's life continues to unfurl, his story serves as a beacon of inspiration for dreamers and doers alike. His journey reminds us that success is not measured solely by accolades or fame, but by the impact we have on the world and the lives we touch along the way.

In Bryan Cranston, we find not just a consummate artist, but a guiding light whose legacy will endure for generations to come. And as we eagerly await the next chapter in his remarkable tale, we are reminded of the power of resilience, creativity, and unwavering determination to shape our destinies and leave a lasting mark on the world.

In the ongoing narrative of Bryan Cranston's life, each chapter unveils new depths of his artistry, resilience, and profound impact on the world around him. From his early struggles to his meteoric rise to stardom, Cranston's journey embodies the quintessential American Dream – a testament to the transformative power of talent, hard work, and unwavering dedication.

With every role he inhabits, Cranston delves deep into the psyche of his characters, crafting performances that resonate with authenticity and emotional depth. Whether he's portraying the morally conflicted Walter White or the towering figure of Lyndon B. Johnson, Cranston's ability to breathe life into complex personas captivates audiences and leaves an enduring imprint on the cultural landscape.

Yet, Cranston's influence extends far beyond his work on stage and screen. Through his philanthropy, advocacy, and commitment to social justice, he has become a beacon of hope and inspiration for countless individuals around the globe. From championing children's safety initiatives to raising awareness about environmental conservation, Cranston's efforts to make a positive impact reflect his profound sense of compassion and empathy.

As the narrative of Cranston's life continues to unfold, it serves as a reminder of the boundless potential that lies within each of us. His story inspires us to pursue our passions relentlessly, to embrace challenges as opportunities for growth, and to strive for excellence in all that we do.

In Bryan Cranston, we find not only a masterful performer but a true Renaissance man – a visionary whose artistry, integrity, and humanity transcend the confines of the entertainment industry. And as we eagerly anticipate the next chapter in his extraordinary journey, we are reminded that the greatest stories are those that inspire us to dream, to create, and to make a difference in the world.

In the unfolding narrative of Bryan Cranston's life, each chapter adds depth to the story of a man who embodies resilience, creativity, and unwavering determination. From his early days struggling to make ends meet to his ascent to the pinnacle of Hollywood success, Cranston's journey is a testament to the transformative power of perseverance and passion.

With every role he takes on, Cranston immerses himself fully, bringing to life characters that resonate with audiences on a profound level. Whether he's portraying the enigmatic Walter White or the formidable Lyndon B. Johnson, Cranston's performances are marked by an authenticity and depth that leave an indelible mark on the viewer's psyche.

Beyond the glitz and glamour of Hollywood, Cranston's impact extends into the realm of philanthropy and activism. He uses his platform to advocate for causes he believes in, from children's safety initiatives to environmental conservation efforts. Through his actions, Cranston demonstrates a commitment to making the world a better place, one role at a time.

As the chapters of Cranston's life continue to unfold, his story serves as an inspiration to aspiring artists and dreamers everywhere. His journey reminds us that success is not defined by accolades or wealth, but by the impact we have on others and the legacy we leave behind.

In Bryan Cranston, we find not just a talented actor, but a beacon of hope and possibility. And as we eagerly await the next chapter in his remarkable journey, we are reminded of the power of perseverance, passion, and the belief that anything is possible when you dare to chase your dreams.

In the tapestry of Bryan Cranston's life, each chapter is woven with threads of resilience, creativity, and an unwavering commitment to excellence. From his humble beginnings to his rise as one of Hollywood's most celebrated actors, Cranston's journey embodies the quintessential American story of perseverance and triumph.

With each role he undertakes, Cranston transcends the boundaries of performance, immersing himself fully in the lives of his characters and bringing them to life with unparalleled depth and authenticity. Whether he's portraying the complex anti-hero of Walter White or embodying the towering presence of Lyndon B. Johnson, Cranston's performances resonate with audiences, leaving an indelible mark on the cultural landscape.

Yet, Cranston's impact extends far beyond the silver screen. Through his philanthropy, advocacy, and humanitarian efforts, he leverages his platform to make a positive difference in the world. From supporting children's charities to championing environmental conservation, Cranston demonstrates a profound sense of compassion and empathy that inspires others to take action.

As the chapters of Cranston's life unfold, his story serves as a beacon of hope and inspiration for aspiring artists and dreamers everywhere. His journey reminds us that success is not measured by fame or fortune, but by the lives we touch and the legacy we leave behind.

In Bryan Cranston, we find not only a masterful actor, but a true visionary whose passion, resilience, and humanity continue to inspire generations to come. And as we eagerly anticipate the next chapter in his extraordinary tale, we are reminded of the power of perseverance, creativity, and the enduring belief in the limitless potential of the human spirit.

With every turn of the page, Bryan Cranston's narrative unfolds like a captivating drama, rich with moments of triumph, adversity, and profound transformation. From his formative years marked by struggle and uncertainty to his ascent to the summit of Hollywood acclaim, Cranston's journey serves as a testament to the resilience of the human spirit and the boundless possibilities of relentless determination.

As he steps into the shoes of his characters, Cranston breathes life into each role with a rare blend of intensity and vulnerability, capturing the essence of their humanity with unparalleled depth and authenticity. Whether he's navigating the moral complexities of Walter White or embodying the towering presence of Lyndon B. Johnson, Cranston's performances leave an indelible imprint on the hearts and minds of audiences around the world.

Yet, Cranston's impact transcends the silver screen, as he uses his platform to champion causes close to his heart and effect positive change in the world. Through his philanthropy, advocacy, and unwavering commitment to social justice, he inspires others to join him in the fight for a brighter, more compassionate future.

As the chapters of Cranston's life continue to unfold, his story serves as a beacon of hope and inspiration for dreamers and doers alike. His journey reminds us that greatness is not defined by the heights we reach, but by the depths of our character and the mark we leave on the world.

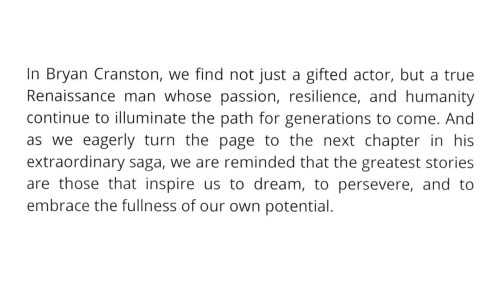

In Bryan Cranston, we find not just a gifted actor, but a true Renaissance man whose passion, resilience, and humanity continue to illuminate the path for generations to come. And as we eagerly turn the page to the next chapter in his extraordinary saga, we are reminded that the greatest stories are those that inspire us to dream, to persevere, and to embrace the fullness of our own potential.

In the unfolding narrative of Bryan Cranston's life, each chapter reveals layers of complexity, depth, and unwavering determination. From his humble beginnings to his meteoric rise to stardom, Cranston's journey embodies the essence of the American Dream—a testament to resilience, hard work, and the pursuit of one's passion.

With every role he takes on, Cranston delves deep into the psyche of his characters, infusing them with a raw authenticity and emotional depth that resonate with audiences worldwide. Whether he's portraying the enigmatic Walter White or the indomitable Lyndon B. Johnson, Cranston's performances are a masterclass in the art of storytelling, leaving an indelible impression on viewers long after the final curtain falls.

Beyond the glitz and glamour of Hollywood, Cranston is a beacon of compassion and empathy, using his platform to advocate for social causes close to his heart. From supporting children's charities to championing environmental conservation, Cranston's dedication to making a positive impact on the world is as profound as his talent on screen.

As the chapters of Cranston's life continue to unfold, his story serves as an inspiration to dreamers and doers everywhere. His journey reminds us that with passion, perseverance, and a willingness to embrace life's challenges, anything is possible.

In Bryan Cranston, we find not just a gifted actor, but a true visionary whose artistry, integrity, and humanity continue to enrich the world around him. And as we eagerly anticipate the next installment in his remarkable saga, we are reminded that the greatest stories are those that inspire us to reach for the stars and never give up on our dreams.

In the tapestry of Bryan Cranston's life, each new chapter unfolds with a blend of intrigue, passion, and unwavering dedication. From his formative years shaped by adversity to his emergence as a towering figure in the entertainment industry, Cranston's journey is a testament to the power of resilience, creativity, and unyielding determination.

With every role he undertakes, Cranston breathes life into characters with a rare combination of depth, nuance, and authenticity. Whether he's portraying the morally complex Walter White or bringing historical figures like Lyndon B. Johnson to vivid life, Cranston's performances captivate audiences and leave an indelible mark on the cultural landscape.

But Cranston's influence extends far beyond his work on screen. He is a passionate advocate for causes that matter deeply to him, from children's safety initiatives to environmental conservation efforts. Through his philanthropy and activism, Cranston demonstrates a commitment to making a positive impact on the world and inspiring others to do the same.

As the narrative of Cranston's life continues to unfold, it serves as a source of inspiration for dreamers and achievers everywhere. His story reminds us that greatness is not defined by success alone, but by the resilience, compassion, and integrity with which we navigate life's challenges.

In Bryan Cranston, we find not just a talented actor, but a true Renaissance man whose passion for his craft and dedication to making a difference set him apart. And as we eagerly await the next chapter in his extraordinary journey, we are reminded of the transformative power of perseverance, creativity, and the relentless pursuit of one's dreams.

In the ever-evolving narrative of Bryan Cranston's life, each successive chapter adds depth, complexity, and a renewed sense of purpose. From his early struggles to carve out a place in the world of entertainment to his meteoric rise as a revered actor and advocate, Cranston's journey is a testament to resilience, authenticity, and the unwavering pursuit of excellence.

With each role he inhabits, Cranston immerses himself fully, bringing a profound humanity and depth to his characters that transcends the confines of the screen. Whether he's embodying the transformation of Walter White in "Breaking Bad" or channeling the commanding presence of Lyndon B. Johnson on stage, Cranston's performances resonate with audiences, leaving an indelible impression long after the curtain falls.

Yet, Cranston's impact extends beyond his acting prowess. He is a passionate advocate for social causes, using his platform to shine a light on issues ranging from children's welfare to environmental conservation. Through his philanthropy and activism, Cranston inspires others to join him in creating positive change and leaving a lasting impact on the world.

As the chapters of Cranston's life unfold, his story serves as a beacon of hope and inspiration for aspiring artists, activists, and dreamers everywhere. It reminds us that success is not measured solely by accolades or fame, but by the depth of one's character and the legacy they leave behind.

In Bryan Cranston, we find not just a talented actor, but a compassionate and driven individual whose dedication to his craft and commitment to making a difference continue to shape the world around him. And as we eagerly anticipate the next installment in his remarkable journey, we are reminded of the transformative power of authenticity, resilience, and unwavering determination.

Printed in Great Britain
by Amazon